Abraham Shrub

SPARKLE WINKLE

UNDERSTANDING THE SIGNIFICANCE OF CELEBRATION OF FATHER WHILE ALIVE

By

Abraham Shrub

Table of Contents

INTRODUCTION..4

WILLIAM'S FAMILY..8

THE START OF PARENTHOOD..............................16

KID UPBRING..22

FAMILY ISSUE..26

SIGNIFICANCE OF A DAD IN A CHILD'S LIFE...30

FATHER'S RELATIONSHIP....................................32

FATHERS CLOSE TO HOME TURN OF EVENTS 36

FESTIVITY OF FATHER'S DAY.............................38

TRIBUTE TO MY BELOVED FATHER..................44

INTRODUCTION

There are two accounts of when the primary Dad's Day was praised. As per a few records, the main Dad's Day was commended in Washington State on June 19, 1910. A lady by the name of Sonora Savvy Dodd thought of regarding and praising her dad while paying attention to a Mother's Day message at chapel in 1909. She felt like moms were getting all the recognition while fathers were similarly meriting a day of commendation (She would presumably be disappointed that Mother's Day actually gets the vast majority of consideration).

Sonora's father was truly a man. William Shrewd, a veteran of the nationwide conflict, was left a single man when his significant other kicked the bucket while bringing forth their 6th youngster. He proceeded to bring up the six kids without anyone else on their little homestead in Washington. To show her appreciation for all the difficult work and love William provided for her and her kin, Sonora figured there ought to be a day to give recognition to him and different fathers like him. She at first proposed June fifth, the commemoration of her dad's demise to be the assigned day to observe Father's Day, however because of some awful preparation, the festival in Spokane, Washington was conceded to the third Sunday in June.

The other story of the principal Father's Day in America happened as far as possible on the opposite side of thc country in Fairmont, West Virginia on July 5,

1908. Elegance Brilliant Clayton proposed to the clergyman of the neighborhood Methodist church that they hold administrations to celebrate fathers after a destructive mine blast killed 361 men.

While Father's Day was praised locally in a few networks the nation over, informal help to make the festival a public occasion started very quickly. William Jennings Bryant was perhaps of its staunchest defender. In 1924, President Calvin "Quiet Cal" Coolidge suggested that Father's Day become a public occasion. In any case, no authority move was made.

In 1966, Lyndon B. Johnson, through a leader request, assigned the third Sunday in June as the authority day to observe Father's Day. Nonetheless, it was only after 1972, during the Nixon organization, that Father's Day was formally acknowledged as a public occasion.

Very much like history has shown the significant of festivities of fathers, this book is extra that father are intended to praised constantly not simply on father's day

CHAPTER 1

WILLIAM'S FAMILY

William's families are appreciates and love to connect with locally. Very much like each and every other African family, known to be broadened, where your aunt or uncle can visit with practically no type of warning and will be free to remain as long as they need to. In most African home you can't actually tell their religion since they could have an uncle who is a Christine or a sibling who is Muslim and the extraordinary granddad who could have moved from one town to the next in light of the fact that he was an IFA cleric or in the family there is a prophet they love.

"Man is known to be polygamy in nature" this can be alludes to a motto, frequently said by the senior lady to little kids, in other to continuously get their brain ready. Incase their better half carried one more lady to the family for marriage. William's family is a polygamous family, made of two spouses and nine kids. The youngsters are comprised of six young men and three young ladies; all informed and have a degree close by with different abilities like baking, catering and so forth.

Mr. Williams and his spouses isn't a degree holder. He just has a lesser optional school declaration. In the Nigerian arrangement of training, the framework is separated into grade school; optional school which can be alludes to as school. Comprehensive of junior optional school and senior auxiliary school both finished in six years. Three years for junior optional school and three years for senior auxiliary school and afterward college which then meet all requirements for single guy in degree. He was unable to proceed is schooling in light of the fact that the parent isn't light to manage the cost of his schooling, then, at that point, he turned into a nonconformist.

After certain years, one of his uncles who lives in the city came to the town to visit his parent and it was examine with him on the off chance that he can take William with him to gain from is exchange. After enough conversation Ayoola the uncle to William chose to take him to the city, but before their flight, William's parent counsel their kid to continuously be submissive to his uncle and learn well in other to accomplish a more prominent level.

Upon the arrival of flight, William sobbed like a child and considered who will deal with his parent. The family is made of three youngsters, two young men and a young lady. The sister to William is hitched and the oldest child is as of now in the city with one of their nearby uncle, so Williams was the only one aiding his parent.

Mr. and Mrs. Ade will miss their youngster to such an extent. The mother packs his effects into the vehicle, Mr. Ade and Ayoola talk about for quite a while William continue to embrace the mother as though he would rather not leave. In the end they move to the vehicles and afterward withdraw. Mr. and Mrs. Ade didn't leave the sight until they quit seeing the vehicles

CHAPTER 2

THE EXCURSION TO THE CITY.

William left the city with his uncle, he was loaded up with tears and dishearten while his parent then again were loaded with lament on how they can't bear to send their kid to school. They trust and supplicated he will track down favor in the city. Williams implore and promises that none of his kid will at any point be a nonconformist, that he most do everything in his ability to progress and send his youngsters to school. In the Nigeria certain gaining tertiary training, resembles nothing to joke about, it give you an edge among your matches and, surprisingly, carried more regard to the family. He was unable to fault his parent since he knows how they want to advance with his review.

Battles proceed, when William joined his uncle in the vehicle business in Lagos Nigeria. Lagos isn't something very similar with where he came from where they are fewer individuals, less traffic and less business exercises. He understood how the entire house hold get up promptly in the first part of the day to arranged and rush down for work.

Business start appropriately the second day they return to Lagos, and keeping in mind that they were en route to the workplace, the uncle gave him a few set down guidelines, that they are some of the time he won't be following to work, that assuming he noticed, he will perceive the way everybody get up so right on time to plan for work. He said, it must be that way since getting up late would result to getting late to the workplace which could involves burning through four hours or more in rush hour gridlock prompting deficiency of cash. He them say punctuality is the way to progress.

William keeps on gaining exchange from his uncle, during the time he was looked by changed difficulties, but he was known for focused, persevering and reliable. His uncle loves him such a lot of that he causes him to be responsible for the everyday running of the business while he handles different exercises connecting with the business.

After numerous long stretches of speculation, he claimed a business and considered beginning a family.

He chose to look for exhortation from his uncle which he was exceptionally blissful about the turn of events.

William headed out to the town to illuminate his parent about the welcome turn of events. The parent was dependably cheerful about how effective their kid has become and how he commits his time and cash on their government assistance. Each time he goes for visiting the residents are consistently glad to see him regardless of whether they don't know about his appearance, he ensure he visit them and give everybody cash or gift he brought from the city.

Before long, the wedding was led; the parent organized in getting an excellent young lady from a decent family All the wedding planning was managed absent a lot of postponement and after the wedding William and spouse move to the city.

CHAPTER 3

THE START OF PARENTHOOD

Entering parenthood is an organic ocean change in a man's life unheard of since pubescence. Beginning half a month after labor, testosterone levels lower as prolactin, vasopressin, and different chemicals increment, reworking a man's mind to set him up for parenthood.

The early phases of parenthood can invigorate. You're at a great time where you're going to enter one more phase of your life. That stage is called, Parenthood. Assuming you're new to this stage, I need to say congrats. While it tends to be cheerful and invigorating, the expectation can likewise be distressing and tedious. The way that you're going to become a dad for the absolute first time, you might be contemplating whether you're even prepared for this huge obligation. You likewise might be contemplating whether you will be a decent father. I'm here to tell you, you're similarly really prepared.

Life right now will be invigorating, blissful, cheerful, and perhaps mitigating. Simultaneously, it will be troublesome, testing, focused, miserable, and restless. You currently have a child to care for. Your youngster must be taken care of, washed, put to bed, changed, and made to specialist for efforts, and so on.

It could be a lot to ponder, yet it should be finished. As a dad, you should do your part and do your fair share. You have 9 months to consider it. Assuming you need to understand books, online journals, watch recordings, make it happen.

Different idea at the forefront of his thoughts, he dread to be a bombed father, hearing the news his significant other was pregnant. That evening they couldn't rest, him and the spouse pondered what to do, to acquire information on the new way, but they cheer over how God has helped them.

After some week Mr. Williams was called by one of their work from the medical clinic, informing him concerning the spouse wellbeing, he was crushed thinking about what the issue could be. On arriving, he was coordinated to the specialist's office, he was their family specialist and them after some collaboration, and he informed him that the spouse has an unsuccessful labor. He was so befuddled then specialist said it was because of stress.

Joke was a dealer and he needed to help her significant other by all means since he is as yet battling with his business. So often she needs to go to the market to get the merchandise, conveying it from one spot to the next and furthermore taking care of clients. The specialist offer a guidance to the both particularly the spouse not to permit Joke to accomplish any upsetting works for the present.

Once more, after certain years she took in and afterward additionally prompted premature delivery. Mrs. Joke has series of postponements, which make the families on the loose to be stressed as they have enjoyed just about seven years in the marriage with no issue.

The families particularly both parent of couples were becoming stressed over their condition. In the African setting particular the Yoruba setting, the main arrangement will be going briefly spouse. Since there is nothing similar to court wedding the entire cycle will be straightforward and simple. Mr. William was guidance to get a second spouse which he in the long run sticks to obviously with the assent of the wife.

They wedding for the subsequent spouse were directed in a tranquil way and she likewise moved to the city. In less than one year the subsequent spouse was pregnant and later put to birth precisely nine months. Everybody was blissful and the service for the youngster was led. The kid was a kid given a local name Adesina', everybody celebrated with the family.

Following two years, Ajoke got pregnant and at last brought forth twins. The entire more distant family overall was blissful and this required the large festival and celebration. Williams was so blissful, after so long his dearest spouse in the end became a mother.

As the year passes, the quantity of kids expanded, until they got to nine in number.

CHAPTER 4

KID UPBRING

The manner, in which one conducts himself as an individual and how he acts in circumstances great and terrible, relies a ton upon the manner in which he has been raised. A large portion of one's character qualities are gained during youth. How one thinks and acts is formed by the manner in which he has been raised, which is the reason guardians play a vital part to play in a kid's turn of events. Nurturing is tied in with helping kids to separate between the right and some unacceptable, making them competent, and supporting their profound, social, and scholarly turn of events. For the youngsters' childhood to be sound, the guardians need to commit sufficient opportunity to them, embrace the correct approaches to educating or directing them, and establish a climate helpful for the kids' turn of events.

William and spouses had a go at everything in their ability to prepare their kids to have a superior life, But there are times they battle with finance. He attempted has much as conceivable to paid their school fess at has when due, couples with the reality he has different kids he is preparing in school.

Mr Ayoola turned out to be sick and he was hurried down to the clinic for clinical consideration. Following a multi-day he drops with practically no substantial disease. Hearing the miserable news the whole family ended up being enraged and upset. He abandoned four youngsters with a spouse; whom turned into Williams' liability.

There are so often William battle with monetary, once in a while he went however much taking credits from bank in traded with properties. He reached the place that he was unable to try and get a couple of shoes all in view of penances and dread that the youngsters and spouse will endure assuming that he wouldn't take do his obligations.

The Williams are being regarded in the general public not on the grounds that they are rich or the most trustworthy individuals in the general public. The youngsters attempts however much as could be expected to continuously carry great names to the family, they succeed well in their review and well act inside and outside the local area, dissimilar to certain kids that doesn't have a decent nurturing and make trouble locally. He is constantly worried about the companions to the youngsters since he accepts kids learn quicker among their friends.

CHAPTER 5

FAMILY ISSUE

There is consistently a terrible side of the family. There was a period the spouses and kids started furious with their father, they terms him father Christmas since they accept he spend more to more abnormal than home, that he isn't giving them more true to form.

The spouses accepts with his status locally, they ought to have huge business and venture, they accept they just have little of everything, that following quite a while of penances with him he was unable to take legitimate consideration of them. In like manner the kids they contrasted their self and different companions, they figure they need more in their financial balance, they think their mates are having business and them also are not little to have.

Most time William get this way of behaving from the spouses and kids, there was a day he scope one the youngsters and out of irritation he told her, that the kids won't really have acquire his property he said after his demise will take all his venture to the halfway house and give other part to the penniless individuals in the general public.

The kids understands what their dad can do, hearing that proclamation frequently and frequently from him, the whole youngsters as of now has the man set of taking care of business of their own.

Both the female and male youngster battle for them self, they put additional work in anything they are doing as opposed to relying upon their dads riches.

Before the majority of them moved on from school, they have organization and business they adventure into; however they actually demand cash from their dad. Some of the time the dad felt the kids are not thankful.

Sparkle Winkle

CHAPTER 6

SIGNIFICANCE OF A DAD IN A CHILD'S LIFE

Anybody can father a youngster, yet being a father takes a lifetime. Fathers assume a part in each kid's life that can't be filled by others. This job can to a great extent affect a kid and assist with forming that person into the individual they become. Mr. William attempts however much as could be expected to prepare the youngsters in the method of God, he generally advised them to continuously recall God in all that they do and when they are making a trip might be going to class. They all school in the west piece of the nation however an alternate locale from Lagos State. Each time the kids are going out their sight, they generally advises the memorable youngsters "the offspring of what their identity is and consistently make a point to keep out for inconvenience". The kids subtly terms this as father's statement, is pretty much like an unmistakable advantage, it drive them to constantly endeavor and be well act any place they track down themselves.

CHAPTER 7

FATHER'S RELATIONSHIP

Father's impact who we are inside, yet the way that we have associations with individuals as we develop. The manner in which a dad treats his kid will impact what the person searches for in others. Companions, sweethearts, and life partners will be in every way picked in view of how the youngster saw the significance of the relationship with their dad. The examples a dad sets in the associations with his youngsters will direct the way that his kids relate with others.

FATHERS DAUGHTER RELATIONSHIP

Little kids rely upon their dads for security and basic encouragement. A dad shows his little girl what a decent connection with a man is like. On the off chance that a dad is cherishing and delicate, his little girl will search for those characteristics in men when she's mature enough to start dating. In the event that a dad is solid and brave, she will relate near men of a similar person.

Mr Wiliam attempted however much as could reasonably be expected to give all that the female kids need, e gave them without asking, from adolescence he let them in on what each they need he will accommodate them.

There was time he went out for work he purchased fabric for two of his female kids. On returning home, he returned home and afterward acknowledged how tight and little the material were. Starting there he quit getting them fabric rather gave them stipend for garments.

FATHERS AND SON RELATIONSHIP

Not at all like young ladies, who model their associations with others in view of their dad's personality, have young men modeled themselves after their dad's personality. Young men will look for endorsement from their dads from an extremely youthful age. As people, we grow up by copying the way of behaving of everyone around us; that is the manner by which we figure out how to work on the planet. On the off chance that a dad is mindful and approaches individuals with deference, the young man will grow up much the equivalent. At the point when a dad is missing, young men shift focus over to other male figures to set the "rules" for how to act and make due on the planet.

CHAPTER 8

FATHERS CLOSE TO HOME TURN OF EVENTS

Fathers, similar to moms, are support points in the improvement of a kid's personal prosperity. Kids shift focus over to their dads to set out the guidelines and implement them. They likewise shift focus over to their dads to give a sense of safety, both physical and profound. Kids need to do right by their dads, and an elaborate dad advances internal development and strength. Studies have shown that when fathers are friendly and steady, it incredibly influences a youngster's mental and social turn of events. It additionally imparts a general feeling of prosperity and self-assurance.

Sparkle Winkle

CHAPTER 9

FESTIVITY OF FATHER'S DAY

Fathers are likewise human and they go through secret battle, that they don't maintain that their youngsters should know off. The kids shouldn't see each obligation as their obligations rather they ought to be valued in every last ways. Kids ought to figure out how to petition God for their parent, don't request things legitimately asked with deference and habits. Having it at the rear of your brain that one day you likewise are arriving at that phase of nurturing. You probably won't be sufficiently rich to purchase your dad a car, built or purchase a house rather there are series of ways the kids value their folks in their own little manner.

One of them is kids frequently commending their dad on father day. They for the most part prepare cakes and enrich the house and seats given a decent deco to the house wraps up. They additionally orchestrate surprised birthday celebration close by with present like fragrances, wristwatch, garments and so forth intermittent and haphazardly trade of present

Saying 'sorry' while you are off-base is likewise a manner by which a kid utilized in valuing his dad. Each time she irritated his dad she was sorry then followed by serving him his favorite food; this is one way one of the kids utilizes.

Something else is dependably let your dad know how attractive he is, appreciate him subsequent to dressing, cause him to comprehend that he is your main ally and most noteworthy pal you have in the life.

Mr. William has been enduring arteritis none of the family knew about, he however is the ordinary torments he in all actuality do get like all other times. He chose to go to the emergency clinic and the specialist encourages him to go for a medical procedure. He took him some time before he closed, during that period is circumstance deteriorates to the point he was unable to work upstanding, he is just at one spot. At times he utilizes strolling sticks to help his self. The whole family where terrified of his condition, after certain months he found a way the bolding ways to perform the medical procedure.

The medical procedure was fruitful, everybody was blissful particularly the youngsters, that their dad return security to the house. Following three days span, during Morning Supplication, the dad asks close by with the kids and told the most youthful of the young men he need to rest. The oldest child returned to actually look at him and acknowledge he was relaxing.

The declaration of his flight was made and his burial service was led quickly with additional deferral. The whole family and neighborhood were miserable; certain individuals think they lost a dad, a few sees is a partner. The people group and the whole family later concede the reality they misfortune a cheer provider in the general public.

After his passing he composed a will and the legal counselor read a lot of the properties where given to his family which incorporate the youngsters, 10% where given to his siblings while half of the 10% where given to the shelter home and the other half to the poor in the general public.

The kids were brimming with shock, how he generally reproves them, not realizing he has ailment he has been sustaining this years. They all vibe culpability and sorry for the manner in which they have treated believing that he doesn't have their current advantage.

They supposed assuming that they were offering more chance to be with him, they would have valued him more. They all petition God for his flight, and tears roll down from their appearances.

CHAPTER 10

TRIBUTE TO MY BELOVED FATHER.

Precisely one year, the family led recognition for their beautiful spouse and father and heart felt message was composed by one of them;

It's been 1years now since I last saw you, my heart actually cries even today, A couple of year prior July 20, 2021 you left this life. Presently seemingly forever a year prior, July that day won't ever be forgotten similarly as you won't ever be neglected. You are in my heart, my brain, and my contemplations and, surprisingly, in my requests. I miss u such a lot of daddy. My heart actually breaks every day, how I miss you such a lot of daddy, I realize you have been with me tossed out each time you've been with us all. You've sat close to me at least a time or two; yes we've talked, even contended a bit however I felt your hand on my shoulder when things got extreme to manage. I heard your uplifting statements, even heard your reproving.

Indeed father, I do luv you as we as a whole do, I miss you horribly yet we know in our souls you are at long last torment free and cheerful. We have just recollections of the relative multitude of great times we had together yet your soul will live on in our souls. You gave such a lot of pleasure to this family all the more then; at that point, you'll at any point be aware. You would be so extremely pleased with you are extraordinary grandkids two and two of whom you didn't get to hold however you saw them being conceived. I know that in my heart. I realize you are looking after us as you generally did. Your family won't ever allow your soul to pass on, you guide us every day of the week, and for that I thank you by and by for the strength you have given us all to faces life as it comes. We will meet again one day, a few of us sooner then others yet when we're together, again it will be a festival of adoration.

You are in my heart and you generally will be, forever, is simply isn’t something similar without you. God just knows and I know, you know how much this family needs you even today as one more year passes. You wouldn't be so cheerful in the event that u knew the amount we really do require you, what every one of us are looking without your solidarity, yet some the way in which I realize you know precisely exact thing is going on, simply petition God for all of us still here on earth I love you daddy as I become older and my wellbeing isn't great, I recollect the day you need home to god, it actually harms following a year, individuals say it gets more straightforward as time passes by however not so much for me. I'm simply so grateful I was adequately fortunate to have you for that multitude of brilliant years we shared such a ton together. you left so quick, that I will always remember I really do in any case recollect the last day we saw each other you're my divine messenger, daddy I miss you definitely, god favor you father, find happiness in the hereafter till we meet again in paradise it will be a particularly cheering day, daddy, I know the amount you cherished being with family particularly during special times of year god favor u daddy, there isn't a day that goes by that I don't think about you, my heart simply breaks I'll constantly be your dear Beti (little girl) I miss you frightfully you are never out of my heart. you were the main part in all my years, there is nobody like you. Favor me to consume rest of my time on earth without you.

www.ingramcontent.com/pod-product-compliance
Lightning Source LLC
LaVergne TN
LVHW020525160826
845677LV00015B/3911